THE ART OF DECISION MAKING

A GUIDE TO CRITICAL THINKING AND PROBLEM SOLVING

SAGE THOMPSON

Copyright © 2024 by Sage Thompson

All rights reserved. No part of this book may be reproduced, stored in a retrieval system, or transmitted in any form or by any means, electronic, mechanical, photocopying, recording, or otherwise, without the prior written permission of the author.

Table of contents

INTRODUCTION 5
    The Significance of Making Decisions 5
SECTION 1 11
CRITICAL THINKING FOUNDATIONS 11
    The Principles of Critical Thinking 11
    Strengthening Your Capacity for Critical Thinking .. 14
SECTION 2 19
THE PROCESS OF MAKING DECISIONS 19
    Understanding When a Decision Is Necessary 19
    Information and Evidence Gathering 21
    Examining Choices and Their Impact 25
SECTION 3 29
METHODS FOR SOLVING PROBLEMS EFFECTIVELY 29
    Frameworks and Models for Problem-Solving 29
    Instruments and Strategies for Making Decisions .. 32
    Making Decisions in Groups 35
SECTION 4 41
OVERCOMING OBSTACLES IN MAKING DECISIONS. 41
    Handling Risk and Uncertainty 41
    Managing Cognitive Biases 45
    Making Inferences from Choices 49
SECTION 5 55

USING CRITICAL THINKING IN PRACTICAL SITUATIONS.. **55**
   Making Personal Decisions..................................... 55
   Professional Settings for Making Decisions............58
CONCLUSION...**65**
   Developing Your Decision-Making Skills..................65

INTRODUCTION

The Significance of Making Decisions

Greetings and welcome to "The Art of Decision Making: A Guide to Critical Thinking and Problem Solving." Decisions influence our lives in every way, from the little to the big. Our capacity to make intelligent, well-informed choices significantly affects our success and pleasure, whether we're selecting a professional route, making a financial investment, or just figuring out what to eat for dinner. This book is meant to serve as your compass, assisting you in making confident and clear decisions in the challenging terrain of decision-making.

Understanding Decisions: Science or Art?

Consider yourself at a fork in the road. Every option that lies ahead is a distinct decision with unique risks and possible results. The process of choosing the course that best fits our objectives and beliefs is known as decision-making. But is this process a science, guided by facts and laws, or is it an art, an intuitive dance with the unknown?

Actually, making decisions involves combining the two. Our capacity to incorporate creativity, experience, and intuition into our decisions is what makes us artists. Understanding cognitive processes, making use of analytical methods, and seeing patterns are all part of the science. By accepting both points of view, we may improve our ability to make decisions and come to decisions that are not only logical but also profoundly aligned with our goals, both personal and professional.

The role of Critical Thinking in Decision-Making

Critical thinking is essential to making wise decisions. This strong ability helps us to assess data, challenge presumptions, and take into account other points of view. By sifting through the noise to find the signal, critical thinking serves as a filter. It gives us the ability to get beyond automatic and impulsive choices, encouraging thoughtful, well-reasoned choices.

Imagine yourself in a position where you have to choose whether or not to invest in a new company. A critical thinker will examine financial accounts closely, study market trends in great detail, and consult with industry experts. They will balance the benefits and hazards, take the long view, and resist giving in to panic or hype. This methodical technique turns ambiguity into well-informed insight, opening the door for long-lasting judgments.

The Mentality of Solving Problems

Life will always include problems. They test us, push us, and eventually propel our development. Navigating the intricacies of decision-making requires cultivating a problem-solving attitude. Resilience, curiosity, and taking a proactive approach to problems are traits of this attitude.

A problem-solving attitude pushes us to see opportunities rather than barriers when presented with challenges. It encourages us to look for novel answers, pose insightful questions, and maintain our flexibility in the face of change. When your team faces a major project setback, for instance, having a problem-solving attitude will encourage you to find the source of the issue, come up with innovative solutions, and carry out a well-thought-out plan of action.

You will learn techniques and resources to improve your critical thinking and problem-solving skills throughout this book. You'll discover how to confidently make choices, handle ambiguity, and transform obstacles into opportunities. You may steer clear of unfulfilling paths and toward a more prosperous existence by becoming an expert decision-maker.

welcome to the path of master decision-making. Now let's get started.

SECTION 1

CRITICAL THINKING FOUNDATIONS

The Principles of Critical Thinking

What's critical thinking?

Consider yourself an adventurer, exploring new ground. Your compass in the informational desert is critical thinking, which enables you to discern between credible and unreliable sources. It involves the methodical process of actively and competently applying, syncing, analyzing, and assessing data. Clarity, accuracy, relevance, and justice are the processes that drive this procedure, which enables you to traverse complexity with insight and precision.

The Mental Capabilities Necessary for Critical Thought

You must develop certain cognitive abilities that serve as your exploration tools if you want to become an expert critical thinker. Among them are:

Analysis: The capacity to dissect complicated knowledge into its component pieces and comprehend how they work together.

Evaluation: Making a distinction between opinion and fact while evaluating the arguments' quality and the reliability of the sources.

Inference: Making intelligent assumptions when needed, but also drawing logical inferences from the data at hand.

Explanation: Make your mental process apparent to others by clearly stating your reasoning and the evidence that supports it.

Self-regulation: Examining your own mental processes, identifying your prejudices, and modifying your ideas appropriately.

Each of these abilities are essential for breaking down issues, analyzing information, and coming to logical conclusions.

Impeders to Efficient Thought

Even the sharpest minds may be impaired by external factors. Among these obstacles are:

Cognitive Biases: Regular mistakes in reasoning influence our conclusions and choices. Examples include anchoring, which occurs when we place an undue emphasis on the first piece of information we come across, and confirmation bias, which occurs when we prefer information that supports our prior ideas.

Emotional interference: making impulsive and illogical decisions when emotions control decision-making.

Social Pressures: Groupthink and cultural norms have the power to impede critical analysis and independent thinking.

Information Overload: It may be challenging to go through the vast amount of information accessible and determine what is factual and important.

To keep your thinking objective and clear, you must identify and go over these obstacles.

Strengthening Your Capacity for Critical Thinking

Methods for Efficient and Reasonable Thought

Applying certain strategies and putting them into practice are necessary to become a skilled critical thinker. Among these methods are:

Socratic Questioning: Asking insightful, thought-provoking questions to elucidate complex concepts and reveal underlying presumptions. This approach promotes a careful analysis of the available data and beliefs.

Mind Mapping: Using images to represent the connections between thoughts and ideas can improve comprehension and memory.

Reflective Thinking: Examining your choices and mental processes on a regular basis to gain insight from the past and enhance your thinking in the future.

These methods provide the groundwork for a methodical way of thinking that can help you solve issues more precisely and imaginatively.

Avoiding Fallacies in Reasoning

Errors in thinking that comprise an argument's logic are known as logical fallacies. Typical fallacies consist of:

Straw Man: Presenting an incorrect picture of a person's position to facilitate an assault.

Attacking the person presenting the argument instead of the argument itself is known as "ad hominem."

False Dilemma: When there are alternative choices, two are presented as the sole ones.

Slippery Slope: Making the unsupported claim that a little action will have large, unfavorable effects.

You can maintain the validity and persuasiveness of your arguments by being aware of and steering clear of these fallacies.

Developing Intellectual Decency

The realization that there is always more to learn and that our knowledge and comprehension are finite is known as intellectual humility. This way of thinking includes:

Open-mindedness: The ability to examine new concepts and viewpoints, even when they contradict your own convictions.

Curiosity: Preserving a genuine enthusiasm for acquiring knowledge and uncovering new insights.

Reflectiveness: Consistently assessing your own opinions and presumptions and being ready to adjust them in the face of fresh information.

You may approach difficulties with a balanced and open mentality by cultivating intellectual humility, which improves your capacity for critical thought and well-informed decision-making.

Making smarter judgments in all facets of your life is made possible by actively honing your critical thinking skills and grasping their fundamentals. Together, let's go off on this intellectual exploration and development adventure.

SECTION 2

THE PROCESS OF MAKING DECISIONS

Understanding When a Decision Is Necessary

Determining Issues and Possibilities

Consider yourself a captain guiding a large ocean. Although the water might be serene, waves and storms are a common occurrence. Knowing when to venture out and when to turn away from approaching danger is the first step in making decisions. Recognizing issues and openings is like recognizing weather patterns. Issues often show up as roadblocks or inefficiencies that interfere with your progress. Conversely, opportunities are like favorable breezes that, if you take advantage of them quickly, may help you advance.

You have to be on the lookout for warning indications of difficulty all the time in order to spot difficulties. Are there any recurrent problems that need attention? Are there any holes in your procedures or resources? Even if opportunities aren't always evident, they may be found if you maintain your curiosity and are receptive to new ideas. Exist any new trends that you might profit from? Exist any places where innovation might result in large gains? It is essential to identify these times in order to make wise decisions.

Determining the Range and Significance of Choices

The next stage after recognizing an issue or opportunity is to describe its extent and possible consequences. This entails asking important questions, such as how pervasive the problem is. Who or what is the decision going to affect? What are the immediate and long-term repercussions?

Imagine a situation where sales at your firm are dropping. Defining the scope may require examining sales data from various goods and areas. The effect may be anything from little tweaks to marketing plans to significant changes to the products that are offered. You can better prepare to handle the problem by having a comprehensive knowledge of its scope and complexity.

Information and Evidence Gathering

Successful Research Methods

Information is your most important tool when making decisions. Consider yourself an archaeologist finding remnants of a long-lost civilization. Good research methods enable you to go farther and uncover the most accurate and pertinent data. Determine what information you need and where to get it first. This might include talking to experts via interviews or studying books, scholarly publications, industry reports, etc.

When gathering data, use a methodical approach. Make a source list and establish specific objectives for the information you want to learn. Make sure you take thorough notes and arrange your research so that it can be easily retrieved and compared. This rigorous technique guarantees that the information you collect is accurate and thorough.

Assessing Information and Sources

Information is not all the same. It is essential to assess the veracity of the data and the authenticity of the sources. See yourself like a detective, carefully examining each hint to ensure its veracity. Consider these important questions: Is the source reliable? Is the data up-to-date and pertinent? Is there proof of a conflict of interest or bias?

Verify the accuracy of the material by cross-referencing it with other sources. Look for consistency among the data points and be cautious around outliers, which might be signs of abnormalities or mistakes. Thoroughly assessing your sources can help you establish a solid basis for well-informed decision-making.

Managing Overload of Information

In the current digital era, information overload is a prevalent problem. Like attempting to drink from a firehose, it's overpowering and might even be fatal. Put quality above quantity in order to handle this. Concentrate on acquiring data that is directly relevant to your choice. To arrange and make sense of massive amounts of data, use tools like mind maps or data visualization software.

To prevent collecting too much information, clearly define the parameters for your research phase. It's crucial to know when to give up as well as where to begin. This methodical technique keeps you from being overwhelmed by details and helps you maintain concentration.

Examining Choices and Their Impact

Innovative Approaches to Solving Problems

Now that you have the data, it's time to create and evaluate possibilities. Imagine yourself as a painter, combining hues to create a work of art. Thinking beyond the apparent answers and taking into account novel options are key components of creative problem-solving. Methods such as mind mapping, brainstorming, and lateral thinking may assist you in discovering new ideas.

Encourage a varied team to share ideas since inspiration may come from a range of viewpoints. Investigate non-traditional alternatives without hesitation; they may contain the answer to your issue.

Weighing Benefits and Drawbacks

Weighing the advantages and disadvantages of each possible choice is the next step once you've compiled a list of them. This procedure is similar to a scale in that it weighs several considerations to identify the optimum course of action. Make a detailed list of the benefits and drawbacks of each choice. Think about things like money, time, practicality, and possible results.

You may quantify the advantages and disadvantages by giving weights to various elements according to their significance. This methodical assessment guarantees that you make thoughtful, well-rounded selections.

Analysis of Situations

Lastly, use scenario analysis to foresee possible outcomes from your choices. Consider yourself a chess player who is planning many moves ahead of time. The process of scenario analysis entails making precise predictions about the possible outcomes of each choice. Think about the most probable, worst-case, and best-case situations.

Analyze how each scenario will affect your objectives and key players. This proactive strategy enables you to plan ahead and create backup plans in case of unforeseen circumstances. Making choices with more knowledge and resilience is possible when you see several scenarios.

You may arm yourself with the knowledge and techniques required to confidently and clearly negotiate the intricacies of life and business by becoming an expert at these decision-making procedures. Let's keep moving forward on this path to become skilled decision-makers.

SECTION 3

METHODS FOR SOLVING PROBLEMS EFFECTIVELY

Frameworks and Models for Problem-Solving

The Six Contemplation Caps

Imagine a group of investigators, each with a different colored hat, each signifying a distinct viewpoint. Edward de Bono created the Six Thinking Hats, a potent framework that encourages people to consider problems from several angles in order to improve their problem-solving skills. Every hat stands for a distinct way of thinking.

White Hat: Concentrates on information and facts.

Red Hat: Accepts feelings and intuition.

Black Hat: Takes risks and possible issues into account.

Yellow Hat: Seek advantages and chances.

Green Hat: Promotes originality and creativity.

Blue Hat: Oversees the thought process and makes sure that every viewpoint is considered.

Individuals and groups may provide well-rounded solutions and get a more thorough grasp of the issue by carefully donning all of the hats.

SWOT Evaluation

Consider yourself an adventurer setting out to discover uncharted land. Your map and compass should be a SWOT analysis, which evaluates your strengths, weaknesses, opportunities, and threats. This framework aids in the assessment of both external and internal variables that may affect your objectives.

Strengths: What are the things you do well? What benefits do you possess?

Weaknesses: What areas need improvement? What might be made better?

Opportunities: What outside circumstances may you take advantage of?

Threats: What roadblocks could stand in your way of success?

A SWOT analysis gives you a strategic picture that will assist you in maximizing your strengths, minimizing your weaknesses, taking advantage of your opportunities, and defending against threats.

The Cycle of PDCA

Imagine an artisan who is always refining his trade to perfection. Plan-Do-Check-Act, or PDCA Cycle, is a four-step process management and improvement method:

Plan: Determine the issue and formulate a plan of action.

Do: Carry out the strategy in a limited manner.

Check: Keep an eye on and assess the outcomes.

Act: If the strategy is effective, carry it out more broadly. If not, continue the cycle with refinement.

Iterative processes ensure that solutions are evaluated and improved for maximum efficacy and promote continuous improvement and flexibility.

Instruments and Strategies for Making Decisions

Trees of Decisions

Consider yourself exploring a deep forest on a branching route, where every fork signifies a decision point. An illustration of prospective options and their probable results is provided by a decision tree. It assists you in methodically examining the effects of every decision.

- Begin with the primary choice at its core.
- Explore other potential avenues.
- Expand much further to provide the ensuing results and repercussions.

Using decision trees, you may analyze possible outcomes, see the roads ahead, and choose the one that most closely fits your objectives and risk tolerance.

Benefit-Cost Analysis

Consider yourself a dealer determining the relative values of several commodities. A quantitative method of decision-making, cost-benefit analysis, compares the advantages and disadvantages of various solutions.

Expenses: Enumerate all of the costs related to each choice.

Benefits: List the benefits and favorable results.

Comparison: Calculate the net value by balancing the overall expenses and benefits.

By ensuring that the choice selected offers the highest net benefit, this analysis aids in the making of logical and financially smart judgments.

Delphi Approach

Imagine a group of knowledgeable elderly people, each offering their expertise to address a challenging issue. The Delphi Method is an organized communication approach that uses many rounds of surveys to collect ideas from an expert panel.

First Round: Individual expert views are shared.

Feedback: The group is given a synopsis of the replies.

Second Rounds: Based on the input, experts modify their positions and progressively come to an agreement.

The Delphi Method, particularly in difficult or unclear situations, maximizes collective knowledge, reduces prejudice, and converges on well-informed conclusions.

Making Decisions in Groups

The Way Group Decisions Work

Imagine a varied group of seamen operating a vessel. Multiple viewpoints, abilities, and experiences are all involved in group decision-making, which may both improve and provide obstacles. Important roles are played by dynamics, including power dynamics, interpersonal connections, and communication styles.

Roles and Responsibilities: Clearly state each member's responsibility to guarantee equitable involvement.

Communication: Encourage polite, honest, and efficient communication to make information exchange easier.

Conflict Resolution: Resolve disputes amicably to preserve unity and concentration within the group.

Comprehending these dynamics facilitates the management of group dynamics and improves cooperative decision-making.

Methods for Establishing Consensus

Picture a choir harmonizing, with each member melting into the overall sound. Finding a solution, even if it isn't everyone's first choice, that the group can agree on is the first step toward building agreement.

Facilitated Discussions: To steer talks and maintain focus, use the aid of impartial facilitators.

Brainstorming Sessions: To provide a variety of solutions, promote candid idea exchange without prompt criticism.

Multi-voting: Let participants choose the alternatives they prefer, therefore reducing the pool of possibilities.

These methods assist organizations in coming to decisions that demonstrate dedication and collective knowledge.

Controlling the Group Mind

Imagine a group of birds flying blindly in one direction. When a group's desire for unity results in bad decisions, it's known as groupthink. To control the groupthink:

Promote Dissent: Create an atmosphere that values inquiry and critical thought.

Diverse Teams: To prevent homogeneous thinking, put together teams with a range of backgrounds and viewpoints.

Devil's Advocate: Designate an individual to purposefully refute concepts and presumptions.

By taking proactive measures to avoid groupthink, you can make sure that choices are robust and well-thought out, using the perspectives of all group members.

By becoming proficient in these methods and approaches for efficient problem solving, you enable both your team and yourself to approach obstacles with assurance, originality, and accuracy. Let's explore these techniques in more detail so you can maximize your ability to make decisions.

40

SECTION 4

OVERCOMING OBSTACLES IN MAKING DECISIONS

Handling Risk and Uncertainty

Understanding Uncertainty vs. Risk

Consider yourself a sailor traveling through unknown seas. Risk is similar to a storm that you can see coming from the horizon; you can make plans for it. On the other hand, uncertainty is like a fog that surrounds your ship and prevents you from seeing forward. Making informed decisions requires an understanding of the distinction between risk and uncertainty.

Risk: conditions in which the likelihood of various outcomes is known or determinable. For instance, there are risks associated with stock market investments that may be quantified using historical data.

Uncertainty: Conditions in which it is not feasible to determine the likelihood of a certain result. Because there are no previous products to set expectations for, there is a great deal of uncertainty when launching a brand-new product in an unexplored market.

You may adjust your decision-making techniques according to whether you're dealing with risk or ambiguity.

Evaluation and Handling of Risk

As an architect, picture yourself constructing a skyscraper. Your blueprints and safety inspections are risk assessment and management, which make sure the building remains sturdy in the face of any dangers. To control risk in an efficient manner:

Identify Risks: Enumerate possible dangers connected to the choice. Think about things like time, money, and possible roadblocks.

Analyze Risks: Consider each risk's effect and probability. Prioritize which hazards need greater attention by using tools such as risk matrices.

Mitigate Risks: Create plans to lessen the possibility or effect of risks that are high on your list of priorities. This might include making backup plans, getting insurance, or diversifying your money.

Monitor and Review: Keep an eye out for emerging hazards in the environment, and make sure your tactics are still working by routinely reviewing them.

By methodically evaluating and controlling risks, you may make well-informed choices that take future difficulties into consideration.

Methods for Determining Under Uncertainty

Consider yourself a chess player against an unexpected opponent. Making judgments in the face of uncertainty calls for adaptability and flexibility. The following are some tactics:

Scenario Planning: Create a number of scenarios based on various hypotheses, then arrange your responses for each. This helps prepare you for a variety of potential outcomes.

Real alternatives analysis: Consider choices as a range of alternatives as opposed to a single, significant commitment. This enables you to adjust when new information becomes available and make small judgments.

Embrace Agility: Be prepared to veer off course when new information becomes available. Agile decision-making procedures, which are popular in software development, may be used to improve responsiveness in a variety of industries.

You may move confidently and adaptably through uncertainty with the help of these tactics.

Managing Cognitive Biases

Typical Cognitive Biases in Making Decisions

Consider yourself a detective working on a challenging case. Similar to red herrings, cognitive biases deceive and mask the truth. The following are some typical biases that influence judgment:

Confirmation bias is the tendency to ignore data that contradicts your prior opinions in favor of information that supports them.

Anchoring Bias: Making judgments by placing an excessive amount of weight on the initial piece of information (the "anchor").

Overconfidence Bias: Making too optimistic conclusions due to an overestimation of your expertise and skills.

Hindsight Bias: thinking you could have foreseen the result of an event after it had already happened.

Identifying these prejudices is the first step in reducing their influence on your choices.

Methods for Reducing Biases

Consider yourself a scientist carrying out a meticulous investigation. Your controls and procedures are your strategies to reduce biases and ensure unbiased and trustworthy outcomes. Here are a few successful tactics:

Awareness and Education: Become knowledgeable about typical cognitive biases and their consequences for both you and your team. Biases may be lessened by awareness alone.

Diverse Teams: To combat individual prejudices, assemble teams with a range of backgrounds and viewpoints. Diverse perspectives have the power to refute presumptions and produce more thoughtful conclusions.

Structured Decision-Making Processes: Make choices by using checklists and frameworks. Organized procedures might assist you in methodically taking into account all pertinent aspects.

Devil's Advocacy: Assign someone to purposefully refute your presumptions and findings. This lessens groupthink and reveals blind spots.

You may draw conclusions that are more logical and impartial by putting these tactics into practice.

Welcoming Diverse Viewpoints

Imagine a council including sage counselors, each contributing distinct perspectives. Accepting several points of view enhances the decision-making process. Here's an efficient way to accomplish it:

Promote Open Communication: Establish a setting where people are at ease expressing their opinions.

Seek Out Different Opinions: Make a conscious effort to get feedback from people with various backgrounds, experiences, and levels of competence.

Think About Other Options: Refrain from choosing the first option that occurs to you. Examine and consider a variety of options before deciding.

Different viewpoints might highlight blind spots and inspire more creative and practical solutions.

Making Inferences from Choices

The Significance of Input and Analysis

Consider yourself an artisan, improving your abilities with practice. You may polish your skills and improve your workmanship by using feedback and reflection as your sharpening stones. After deciding, give yourself some time to consider the procedure and results, as well as to get input.

Seek Constructive Feedback: Actively seek input from stakeholders, impacted parties, and coworkers. Recognize the successes and failures.

Think Back on the Process: Assess the actual decision-making process. Were there any blind spots or biases? To what extent did the frameworks and strategies function?

Record Lessons Learned: Make sure you document the things you learn from each choice you make. This may be a useful tool for making decisions in the future.

Evaluating Results and Acquiring Knowledge from Errors

Consider yourself a coach analyzing a game to enhance performance in the future. Continuous improvement requires analyzing results and learning from errors.

Result Analysis: Examine the differences between the predicted and actual results. Find any differences and comprehend the reasons behind them.

Root Cause Analysis: Examine closely to find the underlying causes of errors. This lessens the chance of making the same mistakes again.

Celebrate Successes: Honor and commemorate wise choices. Recognize the factors that led to the accomplishment and learn how to repeat it.

Ongoing Enhancement and Modification

Assume you are a gardener who is continuously providing care and adjustments to your plants in order to assure their development. To evolve and prosper in a changing environment, one must constantly develop and adapt.

Iterative Improvement: Make constant improvements to your decision-making procedures in response to input and introspection. Over time, little, gradual advancements might add up to big wins.

Adaptability: Remain adaptable and prepared to modify your strategy in light of new facts and situations. Being flexible is essential to being productive and relevant.

Lifelong Learning: Make a commitment to continued education and growth. Continually learn about new findings, instruments, and optimal approaches to problem solving and decision-making.

Establishing a culture that prioritizes ongoing enhancement and adjustment will help you make better decisions more often and consistently provide better results.

Starting this path of conquering decision-making obstacles will give you the flexibility, resilience, and insight required to successfully negotiate the complexity of today's environment. Together, we will go deeper into these chapters to help you become the most competent decision-maker you can be.

SECTION 5

USING CRITICAL THINKING IN PRACTICAL SITUATIONS

Making Personal Decisions

Daily Choices and Long-Term Strategy

Think of your life as a large, elaborate garden. You have a million little choices to make every day, including which plants to water and how to care for them. The decisions you make on a daily basis add up to form your life's path. By using critical thinking, you can ensure that every decision you make is in line with your beliefs and objectives.

Conversely, long-term planning is similar to creating a blueprint for an exquisite garden that will grow over time. It entails defining specific, attainable objectives and the actions required to achieve them. Critical thinking is a useful tool for assessing possibilities, foreseeing problems, and maintaining focus on your goals while making decisions about your profession, finances, or personal development.

Holding Emotion and Logic in Check
Imagine a tightrope walker maintaining a high level of balance. When making decisions, you must strike a balance between passion and reason, just as they must keep their equilibrium to prevent collapsing. Though they may be a useful source of inspiration and insights, emotions can also drive reckless behavior when left uncontrolled. Although logic, which is based on critical thinking, offers structure and clarity, it sometimes ignores the human factor.

Making judgments that are both sensible and genuinely rewarding may be achieved by identifying and combining logic and emotion. For example, weigh the emotional (happiness, family connections) as well as the logical (professional growth, money) advantages of moving to a new place for work.

Applications and hands-on activities

Consider yourself a student at a workshop, eager to put your newly acquired skills to use. To improve your critical thinking abilities in practical situations, use case studies and activities. Let's examine a couple instances:

Case Study: You're organizing a significant acquisition, such as a vehicle purchase. Examine various models critically, taking into account aspects like cost, dependability, and environmental effects. Make an educated choice after weighing the advantages and disadvantages of each option.

Activity: Create fictitious situations to hone your decision-making skills. For instance, let's say you need to organize a trip but have a tight budget. Make a thorough plan that makes the most use of your resources by researching locations, expenses, and activities.

By practicing and honing your decision-making skills, these exercises help you become ready for the challenges of real life.

Professional Settings for Making Decisions

Business Strategic Decision Making

Consider yourself a general organizing a pivotal battle. Making strategic decisions in business is about setting up your organization to succeed in the market. It entails long-term planning, trend analysis, and decision-making to lead your business to prosperity.

Market Analysis: Study the market in-depth to learn about consumer demands, rival tactics, and industry trends. To determine the possibilities, threats, weaknesses, and strengths of your business, use techniques like SWOT analysis.

Resource Allocation: Choose wisely where to allocate the resources of your business. This may be deciding which tasks to put first, how to divide up the money, or how to make the most use of the abilities and skills on your team.

Risk Management: Recognize possible hazards and create plans to lessen them. This might include branching out into new product categories, breaking into untapped markets, or creating backup plans in case of economic downturns.

Guiding and Making Decisions

Consider yourself the ship's captain, directing your crew over choppy seas. Making decisions and being a leader go hand in hand. You must motivate others, exercise courage, and guide your group toward a single objective.

Vision and Communication: Clearly communicate your team's vision and plan. Everyone will comprehend the direction and their part in attaining it if there is effective communication.

Empowerment: Give your team members the power to make decisions in order to empower them. This not only promotes trust but also makes use of a variety of viewpoints and areas of expertise, resulting in more sound conclusions.

Decisiveness: Be ready to make difficult choices, often in the face of insufficient knowledge. Strong leadership is characterized by decisiveness, which allows for quick decision-making in urgent situations.

Ethical Factors in Choosing Professionals

Consider yourself a judge balancing the justice scales. Maintaining integrity, justice, and social responsibility are the three basic goals of ethical considerations in professional decision-making. Every choice you make has moral ramifications that might impact society as a whole, your company, and your reputation.

Integrity: Always make judgments with integrity and openness. Steer clear of conflicts of interest, and make sure that whatever you do complies with your moral principles.

Fairness: Make an effort to reach reasonable and equitable conclusions. Take into account the effects on all parties involved, such as the community, shareholders, staff, and clients.

Social Responsibility: Acknowledge how you affect society more broadly. Make choices that advance social justice, economic growth, and environmental sustainability.

Applying critical thinking to ethical issues guarantees that the judgments you make in your work are not only responsible and principled, but also successful.

We've looked at how to use critical thinking in both personal and professional decision-making in this section of the book. These abilities will enable you to operate with assurance, clarity, and integrity while navigating the difficulties of life. Let's study these chapters in more detail and become experts at making decisions in real life.

CONCLUSION

Developing Your Decision-Making Skills

Including Critical Thinking in Everyday Activities

Think of your mind as a well-tuned instrument that can play melodic, beautiful music. Using critical thinking in your everyday life is similar to playing an instrument with dexterity and ability. You have to make judgments every day; some are little, others are major. Consistently using critical thinking helps you make decisions that are well-considered, well-informed, and compatible with your beliefs and objectives.

Begin by engaging in self-awareness and mindfulness exercises. When you find yourself making choices automatically, catch yourself and take a moment to give your alternatives a closer look. Apply the frameworks and methods you've studied in this book to analyze data, identify hazards, and take into account other viewpoints. These routines will become second nature to you with time, improving your capacity to make wise judgments with ease.

Creating a Mindset for Lifelong Learning

Consider yourself an explorer who is always venturing into new areas and unearthing valuable secrets. Gaining mastery over the art of decision-making requires cultivating a mentality of lifelong learning. Since the world is always changing, it is essential to remain inquisitive and receptive to new information in order to survive.

Make a commitment to lifelong learning by pursuing new opportunities, reading extensively, and participating in group discussions. Accept obstacles as chances to improve and broaden your knowledge. Experiences that include acquiring a new skill, immersing yourself in a foreign culture, or studying a difficult subject all improve your ability to make decisions.

The Path Ahead: Ongoing Development and Enhancement

Imagine yourself traversing broad, breathtaking terrain along a meandering trail. There are many chances for continued development and progress on the path to decision-making mastery. Your progress increases with each step you take, bringing you closer to more knowledge and efficiency.

Consider your choices, both good and bad, on a frequent basis. Examine what succeeded, what failed, and why. Make use of this reflection to improve your tactics and methods. Make sure you are surrounded by peers and mentors who will push you and encourage you to develop together.

Recall that the trip is just as important as the destination. Along the journey, acknowledge and celebrate your successes, but never settle for less. Continue to be dedicated to your career and personal growth, constantly looking to improve your ability to make decisions.

To sum up, developing the skill of decision-making takes a lifetime. Through incorporating critical thinking into your everyday routine, adopting an attitude of constant learning, and making a commitment to continuous development and enhancement, you prepare yourself to face life's challenges with assurance and clarity. Keep in mind that every choice you make along the way will provide you with the chance to improve, learn, and become the finest version of yourself. There is a bright future ahead of you, and you have boundless potential. Accept the trip and become an expert decision-maker.

www.ingramcontent.com/pod-product-compliance
Lightning Source LLC
Chambersburg PA
CBHW050239230526
45470CB00005B/2027